DinOsaurs & Dinner-Ladies

As always, for Noah & Cara – J.D.

First published in Great Britain in 2016 by
Otter-Barry Books
Little Orchard, Burley Gate, Hereford, HR1 3QS

www.otterbarrybooks.com

A catalogue record for this book is available from the British Library.

ISBN 978-1-91095-956-5

Printed in the UK

1 3 5 7 9 8 6 4 2

MIX
Paper from
responsible sources
FSC® C013254

Dinosaurs & Dinner-Ladies

John Dougherty

Illustrated by
Tom Morgan-Jones

Otter-Barry BOOKS

Contents

Dinosaurs & Dinner-Ladies

In dining-halls of long ago
When dinosaurs sat down to dine
Did prehistoric dinner-ladies
Keep them all in line?

"Oviraptor! Put that down!
Those eggs aren't for your lunch!
That's the Nursery class!"

"Oi! You! Stegosauruses!
When I said *put your lunch properly on your plates*,
I meant the ones on the tables!
Not the ones along your spines!"

"Apatosaurus! Don't be daft!
You'll never eat all that…
Oh. You did.
Well, you're a growing lad, I suppose."

"Tyrannosaurus! Eat your lunch, not the infants!"

The dinosaurs are all long dead
Extinct, departed, sadly missed,
But survival of the fittest means
That dinner-ladies
Still exist.

Note to an English Teacher

A poem
Is like a hamster

Small
(Unless it is a long poem
In which case
It is like a large hamster)
And lively
(Unless it is a dull poem
In which case
It is like a sleepy hamster).

Admittedly
A poem has no fur
But it has a life
A life of its own
Given it by the poet
(Who is to the poem
As God to a hamster)

And as a hamster
Does what a hamster
Was made for
So a poem
Does what it
Was written for.

Perhaps, though
The most striking resemblance
Is that you can take a poem
Apart
As you dissect a hamster
To see how it works

But, once you have done so, you find
On putting it back together
That, like a hamster in the same situation
It does not work
Half as well
As it used to.

I Am the Bully

I am the bully with venomous eyes
I am the bully, I am the bully
I seek out a weakness to mock and despise
I am the bully, I am the bully
Twisting the truth into horrible lies
I am the bully, I am the bully
I am the bully

I am the bully with knuckles of stone
I am the bully, I am the bully
I use them for bruising your body and bone
I am the bully, I am the bully
I take what I want and I make it my own
I am the bully, I am the bully
I am the bully

I am the bully who toys with his victim
I am the bully, I am the bully
Making up fake little reasons I've picked him
I am the bully, I am the bully
Leaving him always unsure if I've tricked him
I am the bully, I am the bully
I am the bully

I am the ice in the bully's heart
Cold as a dagger, sharp as a dart
The ice doesn't care who the ice tears apart
You, or the bully

Have You Ever Wondered...?

Have you ever wondered what teachers do
When they've said goodbye to all of you
And you've gone off home with your mum or dad
At the end of a busy day?

They've spent the day being awfully good
Like all of them say that the children should
But when you're not there, their behaviour is BAD
At the end of a busy day.

Mr Da Vellacott stands on the chairs
Mrs Fyfe-Kensington jumps down the stairs

Mrs O'Donnell and Mr McKnight
Go into the playground to quarrel and fight

Miss Williams, Ms Spencer and old Mr Jones
Shout horrible words out, and sometimes throw stones

Ms Wood, who's so stern when she tells off the boys
Runs through the building and makes loads of noise
While Mr Defoe, who in class is so neat
Sticks chewing-gum under the Head Teacher's seat.

And the Head? She's not daft – while her teachers are all
Misbehaving in classrooms and playground and hall
She plays in the toilets, well out of harm's way
When the kids have gone home at the end of the day.

Geoffrey

There was a boy called Geoffrey who was mean to me
    at school.
I don't recall him ever being anything but cruel.
It felt as if he thought that there was nothing
    so delightful
As doing all he could to make my life completely
    frightful.

But if I were to meet him now that we are
    fully grown,
I hope I'd have the dignity to leave the past alone,
To shake his hand forgivingly, and speak to him
    with grace,
Though probably I'd really want to punch him
    in the face.

Slow Reader

sleef ti woh si sihT
daer ot gninraeL
srettel sseltser htiw gniltserW
esnes ekam sdnuos ekam ot gnilgggurtS
dnecsed uoy, rednerrus ni litnU
ecnelis otnI
tsal ta detaefeD
...tebahpla elbisneherpmocni eht yB

The Spelling Bee

I do not think that I shall ever see
A-buzzing merrily from flower to flower
Another creature like the Spelling Bee
Engaged upon its literacy hour.
Instead of honey, it and all its kind
With all the precious nectar they collect
Make words like 'nematode' and 'unrefined'
With pride that every spelling is correct.
Then boastfully they show them to their queen –
But none of them can tell her what they mean.

Dog poetry

A doggy will only write doggerel
He never will literature write
A horse, of course, if it tries to write verse
Will manage it just about right.

But a doggy will only write doggerel.
If he tries to write poems of love
A lady doggy might give him a snoggerel
But will more likely tell him to shove
Off.

Alligator

The Alligator has no patience
And hence no friends and no relatience
They all have long ago deserted
For fear of getting harmed or hurted.
It snaps its jaws and spits with spite
At every small imagined slight
But worst of all, it hates the crime
Of bending words to force a rhyme.

The Alliterative Alligator

The alliterative alligator
lurks languidly, looking like a lazy log
by the bank, beneath the blue
wavy waters, waiting, wanting,
hunting hungrily but unhurriedly,
seeking something satisfyingly savoury.
Suddenly it strikes, snapping, swallowing,
and as its supper sinks
it thinks
for the first time
of a rhyme:
What delicious
Little fishes...

A Slightly Serious Limerick

If ever your heart is in pain
Feeling like it's been hit by a train
I can quite recommend
The love of a friend
To stop it from happening again

Extinction

If I were a dinosaur
looking upwards, and I saw
an asteroid
I'd be annoyed.

If I were a dodo
I should probably think "Oh-oh"
if I saw a lot of sailors being vicious
on the island of Mauritius.

But seeing
as I'm a human being
perhaps I should be more concerned
about all the fossil fuels we've burned.

Luca

There was a young fellow called Luca
Who found, on his foot, a veruca
Which, to his dismay
Would *not* go away –
So he shot at it with a bazooka.

Seeds

A dandelion seed
as the wind blew
came free from its anchor
and flew
to far away
to begin anew

A raspberry seed
felt the blackbird chew
travelled in darkness
made its slow way through
till it came out
in a poo

I'd rather be the dandelion
wouldn't you?

The Handicap

The tube train rattles and batters and clatters along,
    chattering madly
Its clamour a frantic percussion
That drowns the sounds of attempted discussion
Relentlessly pressing the passengers in on themselves
Until, confined in tiny cages, spheres of silence
Like flies encased alive in amber
They sit in solitude, all alone together.

Except for two, whose hands dance excitedly
Fingers flickering like firelight
Palms flashing like silvered signals
Sending carefree words across the carriage
Heedless of the distant unheard rumbling.

The train slows, stops, and one
Hands still dancing
Stands, alights
And as the doors slide shut behind her
She looks at the silent stiff mannequins within
Grins
And through soundproof window and the roar
    of the engine
She says to her friend in words as clear as glass,
"Wouldn't it be terrible to be handicapped?"

She's Beautiful

She talks with her hands
She talks with her fingers and with her smile
She draws in the sand
And she paints on the sky
She's louder than words
She's louder than windows

And oh, she's beautiful
Oh, she's beautiful
Oh, she's beautiful to me

And though she knows we're not the same
It doesn't mean a thing

Because she talks with her hands
She talks without making a sound
She won't understand
About saying goodbye
She's louder than roads
She's louder than railways

And oh, she's beautiful
Oh, she's beautiful
Oh, she's beautiful to me

She doesn't care about the thunder
She doesn't hear the rain
She never notices the silence of the breeze
She doesn't wonder if the way she's always been
    is loss or gain
She lives the way she sees

And she talks with her hands
She talks without raising her voice at all
She lies in the sand
And she plays with the sky
She's louder than words
She's louder than anything you've ever heard

And oh, she's beautiful
Oh, she's beautiful
Oh, she's beautiful to me

Next-Door's Cat

Next-door's cat is a cat with attitude.
It'll take a mile if you give it any latitude.
It's a fat cat that scratches other cats and takes
        their catty food.
I don't like next-door's cat.

Next-door's cat thinks it's something of a hard 'un.
It marches in and prowls around as if it owns my garden
and it leaves its little messes there and never once
        says pardon.
I don't like next-door's cat.

My next-door neighbour stands outside her own
    back door
and she calls and calls her cat until her vocal cords
    are sore
and it looks at me as if to say, "I think I'll just
    ignore her.
I'll go in when I'm ready
and I ain't ready yet."

Because next-door's cat is a cat with attitude.
It'll never show you gratitude.
You can't move it with a platitude.
It's a cat with attitude,
a fat cat with attitude,
a cat that's big and fat and rude.

It's got fat cattitude.

Dogs

I like dogs
like I like people
which is to say:
some, I like a lot
others, not.

People I like include:
the quiet ones
the gentle ones
the cute ones
the happy ones
the friendly ones who bound up to you
and hold out a paw for you to shake.

People I don't like include:
the angry ones
the threatening ones
the aggressive ones
the unnecessarily loud ones
and the ones who say:

      don't worry
      don't worry
      it's fine
      he won't hurt you
      he wouldn't hurt a fly…

Oh

      He's never done *that* before.

Noah's Diary

– What's this? I say, pointing to his red-raw
    graze-streaked elbow.
He grins as he climbs into the bath.
Aw, Dad, that was a great game! Me and Ben,
we were being secret agents, and Alex was the bad guy
and he nearly got away, but then
I grabbed him and I didn't let go, even though
My elbow scraped against the wall, and it was really sore.
– Did you win? I say.
That grin again.
– And what about this one? I ask. What happened
    to your shin?
That was when Oscar tackled me, and I got a penalty
and I scored. It was so cool, Dad, the best goal
    of the whole match.
– Oh yes?
Now tell me, what's that pink bit here
with the green stains all round it?
I was playing in the woods, he says, *and I got stung by a*
    nettle.
– Right, I nod, seeing. So the green stuff would be...
Dock leaf, he tells me. *I rubbed it on like you*
    always say
and it didn't hurt a bit.
– Grand, I say. Well, it'll have done its job.

34

And then I see his hands, and I can't believe
how mucky they are, or how I haven't noticed
    them before.
– How on earth, I say, how on earth
did you get your paws in such a state as that?
His face lights up, the best one yet.
Aw, Dad, it was wicked.
I caught a newt, a real one, in the pond.
I held it, and it crawled on to my hand.
It had an orange tummy, Dad, really, really bright.
I'll catch one tomorrow and show you, if you like.

– I'll look forward to that, I say, but for now
we ought to clean that off, don't you think?
　　Otherwise
where are you going to put all the muck and dirt
from tomorrow's adventures?
He smiles again, that big wide beautiful grin.
Do you think, he says, tomorrow's
going to be as good as today?
– I hope so, I say. I hope all your tomorrows
make you so happy.
And suddenly that smile lights up his face again.
My lovely Daddy! he says, bursting with all the fun
　　he's had.
And before I know it, he's grabbed me
and given me the best kiss ever,
one I'm never
ever
going to try to wash away.

Deuwayne

There was a young lad called Deuwayne
Who found being good quite a strain
So instead he would shout
And wander about
Till he drove all his teachers insane

My Teacher's Always Picking on Me

My teacher's always picking on me
and I don't think it's fair.
She says I drive her up the wall
and leave her tearing out her hair.
I don't know why she hates me
but it's always me who gets the blame.
No matter what's been going on
you'll hear her yelling out my name.

Just 'cos it was me who broke the window
on my very first day at school.
Just 'cos it was me who pushed Samantha Jones
In the deep end of the pool.
Just because I threw a punch at you and missed
and hit the teacher with my fist.
And I don't think it's fair
that my teacher's always picking on me.

Now Emily Green is going to tell on me
and I'll be in detention.
She said I used her brand-new pen
to write a word that she can't mention.

And of course Miss is going to believe her,
just you wait and see.
I bet you I'd have got the blame
even if it actually hadn't been me.

Just 'cos it was me who broke the window
with Tommy Watson's head.
Just 'cos it was me who fed the pigeons
with high-explosive bread.
Just because I flushed the hamster down the toilet.
How was I to know that it would spoil it?
It's never been the same since then.
And the toilet hasn't either.

Just 'cos it was me who broke the window
and made the teacher frown.
Just 'cos it was me who pinched her lighter
and burned the whole school down.
It was just supposed to be a bit of fun,
it could have happened to anyone.
And I don't think it's fair
that my teacher's always picking on me,
my teacher's always picking on me,
my teacher's always picking on me....

I'm going to tell my mum.

Mr Weiner

A teacher, by name Mr Weiner
Declared, 'I have never felt finer!
For I've just packed the kids
Into boxes with lids
And I've posted them, first class, to China…'

Pink

I don't think
that pink
is a colour
that belongs just to one set of people and not the other.

I don't believe I should only enjoy things
that somebody else has decided are boy things.

I think it's absurd that the word that I've heard
in the playground
is all about putting me down
if I don't fall in line with what someone else says are
the ways that I ought to be,
ways that I've got to be,
just 'cos I'm one of those people who learned to pee
standing up,
'cos my equipment is different
from the people they tell me
have no choice except to like everything pink.

No matter whatever they actually think.

Olive Green

Olive Green isn't green.
She's black.
Which means she is brown.

Tunde White is black.
He is brown, too.

Light brown.
Which still counts as black.

Becky Brown is white,
which means a sort of pinky-beige.
When she draws herself, the teacher tells her
to colour her face in using the peach pencil.
Which is odd, as peaches are yellow and red
and she isn't.
But neither is the peach pencil.

Sam Black is white.
He has big brown freckles all over his face.
But they don't count.

I am white, too,
even though I am browner than Becky Brown
and the bits of Sam Black that haven't been disqualified
on the grounds of being freckles.
In the summer I go even browner.
So brown that I am browner than Tunde White
who is light brown
and therefore black.
But even when I am browner than he is
I am still white
and he is still black.

And my mum says my teacher
has olive-coloured skin
even though olives are green
or black
or reddish-brown.
I suppose 'olive-coloured' doesn't mean
the same colour as an olive.

Nor does it mean
the same colour as Olive Green,
who is black,
which means brown.

Stickers

Bradley Baxter got a sticker today
because he only shouted out three times in class
and once in assembly.
I never shouted out at all; I never do.
But I never got no sticker.

Bradley Baxter got a sticker today
because he kept his hands to himself
and never hit no one till lunchtime.
I never hit no one at all; I never do
(except once when Bradley Baxter stuck a pencil in me
     so hard it broke
and I got mad and whacked him one
and got kept in at playtime
and Bradley Baxter got me back after school).
But I never got no sticker.

Bradley Baxter got a sticker today
for being nice to the new kid.
He sharpened his pencil for him.
I was nice to the new kid; I always am.
I showed him where the loos are,
where the dinner queues are,
where the playground is, and who the worst
     teachers are.

More importantly, I told him not to sit in front of
    Bradley Baxter.
I told him not to tell when Bradley Baxter pinched
    his pencil.
I told him not to hit back when Bradley Baxter stuck
    the pencil in him so hard it broke.
I told him not to say a word when Bradley Baxter
    got a sticker for sharpening the pencil he'd just
    broken by sticking it in him.
And I told him, if you're good, and work hard, and do
    what the teachers tell you
you won't get in trouble.
But you'll never get no sticker.

On the Simplicity of Haikus

To appreciate
The haiku, you don't need to
Have a high IQ

Thoughts of a Confused Child Learning about Haikus for the First Time

Five syllables, then
Seven, then five again. Is
This English or Maths?

On the Difficulty of Expressing Affection

Why do I feel shy
Composing this haiku, to
Say, Hi, I like you?

Query

Does it matter
If a haiku's lines are
Slightly too short?

Interactive Haiku

I start with 'knock knock'
You answer, saying, 'Who's there?'
I say 'hike'. You say…?

Haikuedo

Haikus Miss Scarlett
In the conservatory
With the lead piping

Isabel

Isabel told me
She fancied a boy
Who she didn't really know
So she used to lie in wait for him
And stamp upon his toe.

I listened as she told me
And wished, but never said
That she'd give up stamping on his toe
And stamp on mine instead.

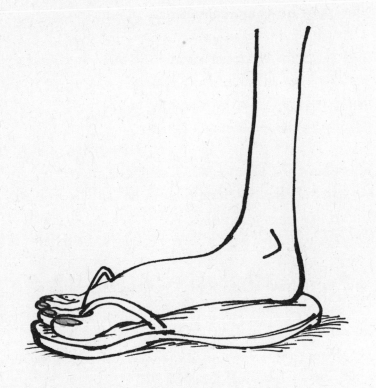

Why Doesn't He Ask Me?

Why doesn't he ask me? Why doesn't he ask me?
My hand's been up for ages, but he doesn't seem
    to see.
And yet he's asked Olivia, Chantel, Jamal and Wayne
when there isn't quite enough between those four
    to make one brain.
And they scratch their heads and rub their chins, and
    then they all agree
that they haven't got the first idea.
Why doesn't he ask me?

Why doesn't he ask me? Why doesn't he ask me?
My hand's been up so long it hurts; he can't have failed
    to see.
He's asked Louise, who's never here; he's asked that
    dozy Janet,
who hasn't grasped this topic – not one bit – since we
    began it.
And now he's asking Jonathan, who acts as if he's
    three
when I know I know the answer.
Why doesn't he ask me?

Why doesn't he ask me? Why doesn't he ask me?
My hand's been up forever! Any idiot could see!
But no! He's asking Robert now, who's screwing up
    his eyes...
...and with one tremendous effort...
...much to everyone's surprise...
...is
  slowly
     coming
     out
  with something logical and wise!
And my teacher's grinning broadly, and he says
    to him, "Well done!
You got it right! Mind you, I'll bet you're not
    the only one."
And to me he says, "Was that what you were going to
    say? I knew
that if no one else had got it, I'd be safe if I
    asked you!"

And I nod and smile as if I'd known the answer
    all along.
Because how can I confess the awful truth?
I'd got it wrong.

Countdown

I'm pretending I am flying towards the moon's
    reflected light
When I see it, then I know my destination is in sight
I am weightless in my spaceship; I can see
    the Milky Way
There are meteors and comets in its heavenly display
I'm feeling this excitement grow, I hope we'll
    be there soon
If I've ever wanted anything, it's to walk upon
    the moon
To stand where Armstrong stood before would be
    so very fine
As Earth relieves that famous day in 1969

Enough pretending! Coming to, I hear the engines
    thunder
And ground control's announcement fills my heart
    with joy and
wonder

We have lift-off!

Face Poem

Faces
Turn up in all manner of places

They have:
Eyes
Which can vary in colour and size
Noses
Which need hankies for wipeses and blowses
Teeth
Which are usually kept underneath   Lips
                    Which are useful for taking sips
                    And eating chips
              With dips

Then there are cheeks, ears, chins
Grins
And the rest of the features
Which make people different
From God's other creatures

Another Face Poem

There are all kinds of faces
Some have glasses and braces
Some are long, some are wide, some are round
Some are dark, some are fair
Some smile brightly; some glare
Some look gloomily down at the ground

Some faces are kind
Some faces are cruel
Some could only be loved by a mother
But whatever the case
We all need a face
To distinguish us, one from another

Brian

Brian loved to play football.
No, that's not quite correct.
And I want to be accurate, from the beginning.
For the thing Brian loved above all about football
wasn't playing the game.
It was winning.

And he usually did
'cos he really was good.
And so everyone wanted to be on his team.
Although nobody liked it when he got too excited,
and the slightest mistake made him scream…

…at somebody else.
It was never his fault.
Even if no one else had been anywhere near
he'd have thought of a way to blame one of us,
make a fuss,
make his contempt for us clear.

Then one day he got
just a little too heated.
When Colin, in goal, let one in, he went mad.
It wasn't as if we were being defeated.
We'd still scored one more than the other team had.
But Brian went off on one.
Called Colin 'useless'!
Colin went scarlet, and silent, and still.
Then suddenly yelled, "You do goals, if you're so
    great,"
and Brian yelled back,
"Fine! I will!"

He stomped to his place
with a look on his face that said,
"Come on, then! Give me the best that you've got!"
And almost immediately, Sam put one past him
with a quite
unremarkable shot.
Brian turned red
and he started to scream at us.
"What were you doing? Defenders! Defence!"
And that was the moment, I think, that we realised
putting up with this didn't make sense.
So we made him stay in there
and we had a great game.
Except Brian. All he did was yell, shout and scream.
But the rest of us all got a turn with the ball
'cos without him we found
we could work as a team.

And we won!
Though it still didn't stop him complaining.
And I thought, as we packed up and went in
        for dinner,
"If there's one thing that spoils a game more
        than a sore loser,
it's a sore winner."

Lonely haiku

Bare autumn branches
The emptiness of lost leaves
The long wait for spring

About Mrs Barry, by Ricky

In the beginning was Mrs Barry.
And Mrs Barry said,
Let there be school!
Then she sat down in her Teaching Chair
And lo, a school arose around her
And it was good
Especially her own classroom.

Then Mrs Barry said,
Let there be a schoolkeeper
To keep everything neat and tidy
And to find my car-keys when they go missing
And to be grumpy with everyone else, but to talk
*   with me about times that only we two*
*   can remember*
And it was so.

And Mrs Barry said,
Let there be life!
As she sat once more in her Teaching Chair
And lo, the school teemed with children
Big children, small children, noisy children,
    quiet children
Children of every shape and size and colour
Filling the halls and the playground and the classrooms
With their laughter and tears, their games
    and their squabbles
Their good days and their bad moods.
And Mrs Barry loved them all.

Most of the time.

About Mrs Barry, by Sarah

Mrs Barry sits enthroned
On her royal blue Teaching Chair.
Her robe is a fuzzy pink cardigan
Her crown is her silver hair.
And a smile and a twinkle light up the wrinkles
In her soft and comfortable skin
As she says,
"Well now, my fine little ladies and gentlemen,
Shall we begin?"

Mrs Barry taught my mother
In olden days when she was young.
Taught her how to sit correctly,
When to speak, or hold her tongue.
And I picture my mum as a little girl
Seeing that twinkling grin,
And hearing,
"Well now, my fine little ladies and gentlemen,
Shall we begin?"

And when Earth's last generation
Lives under a dying sun
And the final class of humanity's children,
Silvery-suited, one by one
Arrive before their teacher,
She'll smile as they all troop in
And say,
*"Well now, my fine little ladies and gentlemen,
Shall we begin?"*

The Invention of the Sandwich

The Earl of Sandwich, called to dinner,
flatly refused to come.
For he said, "If I do, then I won't be the winner
of this game of Shanghai Rum."
"But you're much too thin! And you're getting
        thinner!"
fretted his dear old mum.

The Earl of Sandwich shook his head.
And when his butler came,
he ordered his lunch between slices of bread,
which he ate as he finished the game,
thus inventing a snack which, as everyone said,
should be given the family name.

"Dear Earl of Sandwich, oh, how clever!"
his friend said in surprise.
"I do not think that I shall ever
be half so inventive and wise."
Said the Earl with a smile, "You must never say never,
Dear Duke of Cheeseburger and Fries."

And the Duke thought, "You know, I believe
    the Earl's right!
In fact, I am practically sure
I can think of a snack to bring endless delight,
one the whole world will adore.
But I may need help. I'll discuss it tonight
with Count Max Forjust-Thirtipee Moore"

The Wild Dinner-Ladies

Emergency! Tragedy! Up goes the call.
They're saying that Class 3 are still in the hall!
We just can't believe it! We're silent with shock!
They're still in the hall – ***and it's past twelve o'clock!***
Has nobody warned them? Does nobody care?
Is Mrs Munroe with them? How does she dare?
Has she lost all her senses? Abandoned her brains?
For surely she knows not a second remains
Till the wild dinner-ladies are loosed from their chains!

We run to their rescue – but, no! We're too late.
Through unbreakable glass we must witness their fate.
All the doors have been locked; all the hatches
    are battened
And luckless Class 3 are about to be flattened.
Yes, the fierce dinner-ladies with trolley and tray
Have arrived – and now nothing can stand in their way.

The charge of the trolleys is frightful to see
As the wild dinner-ladies bear down on Class 3.
The children are down! They're all flat on their backs!
And their tummies and faces are crisscrossed
    with tracks,
While Mrs Munroe has been cut clean in half
By the furious, rampaging catering-staff.

Oh, children, take care not to dawdle at all.
When noon comes, be sure that you're out of the hall.
If you're there in their way when they set up for dinner
You'll end up much wider, yet quite a lot thinner.

When Ben Sits Next to Natty

When Ben sits next to Natty
He's too chatty

When he sits next to Joe
He's too slow

When he sits next to Jessie
His work is too messy

When he sits next to Kate
It gets finished too late

When he sits next to Paul
It never gets finished at all

When he sits next to Finn
He doesn't even begin

When he sits next to James
He fools about, and plays games

When he sits next to Ross
He just makes the teachers cross

When he sits next to Jake
He can't stay awake

When he sits next to me
He's as good as can be
He works hard, and does his best
But that's when I'm a pest.

With thanks to Noah & Cara, who helped me write this one

The Real Reasons Dinosaurs Died Out

Velociraptor
Ran with scissors

Tyrannosaurus
Picked on somebody his own size

Iguanadon
Went back after lighting the blue touch-paper

Stegosaurus
Didn't look right and left and right again

Icthyosaurus
Messed about in the swimming lesson

Triceratops
Spotted the plug socket, and thought
"Now, I wonder what would happen if I stuck
my horns in there…?"

And Pterodactyl
Didn't do her homework, once too often
(She had a *very* strict teacher)

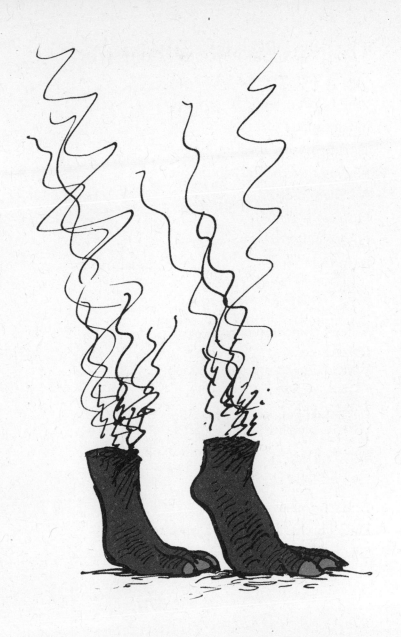

When I Come Home from Work

When I come home from work
Noah is there
Testing his tiny toes and fingers
Waving them happily in the air
And he smiles
His very first smile
His very first
Beautiful
Smile
Is for me
When I come home from work

When I come home from work
Noah is there
Learning to crawl, he peeks out
Into the hall
Sees
It's me
Grins
Ducks back in
When I come home from work

When I come home from work
Noah is there
Red t-shirt between cheeky grin and bare
    bottom
On the top stair
"Hiya, Dad!" he yells
"Come up!"
I do
See the game that he's playing
Kiss his sister too
Gaze at them both till I can't help grinning
The corners of my mouth stuck fast and happy
Half-way up my cheeks
When I come home from work

But one day soon
When I come home from work
Noah won't be there
He'll be out playing football
                 basketball
                     skateboarding
With a friend somewhere

Or
Learning the drums, or playing guitar
Or
Out on his bike, or
driving the car
meeting his girlfriend
staying out late
Working
at school
at his first part-time job
at the rest of his life
and
Someday
Noah won't live here any more

Someday
Maybe
When Noah comes home from work
I'll be there
Playing with my grandchildren
Sitting in Noah's (Daddy's) chair
And I'll smile a wrinkled smile
When Noah comes in

Maybe
      One day
When Noah leaves work, he won't go home
He'll rush to
Wherever I am
Lying, waving my aged fingers helplessly in the air
Waving goodbye
And who knows? Maybe
My very last grin
Will be for him.

Shopping Shock

I saw Teacher in Tesco's, trundling her trolley
Checking the chicken out, fresh versus frozen
And somehow I thought it would be rather jolly
To just sneak a peek at the goods that she'd chosen.

Now, if Mum had seen me, well, she'd have been furious
But she was preoccupied, shopping for tea
And I wasn't being naughty exactly – just curious
I think you'd have done it too, if you'd been me.

'Cos I don't really know all that much about Miss
Where she lives, who her friends are, all that kind of stuff
While she knows the works about me, and I thought, 'This
Might even it up a bit – that's fair enough.'

So I peeked and I poked around, all through
    her shopping
She'd bought herself toothpaste for sensitive teeth
'And no wonder!' I thought, 'Look at all this ice-
    cream!'
Then I lifted the cereal up, and beneath
I found something that came close to making me
    scream....

Oh, finding it shouldn't have been a surprise.
I buy it myself, when I'm shopping with Mum.
But it's shocking to see with your very own eyes
That your teacher buys paper for wiping her bum!

How I wish that I hadn't examined her shopping.
It was stupid and reckless, the wrong thing to do
For now when I see her there's no way of stopping
Myself from imagining Miss on the loo.

Sail Away Between the Pages

I've got a fiction addiction, an absolute conviction
That I need my fix of fiction every night and every day
I've got an actual, intractable hunger for the factual
And there's nothing you can do to make that hunger
    go away

Now the TV and the internet are both good friends
    of mine
I know they have their place and there's no doubt
    they have their time
But when that hunger, that addiction grabs me
    by the throat and rages
The only thing to do is grab a book
And sail away between the pages

Drift away with every word
No matter if the book is
Theoretical or fanciful or practical or joyously absurd
Sail away between the pages
Set a course for new frontiers
And everything that never really mattered
    in the first place
Simply disappears

So if I ever need a friend indeed, I find one in
    the books I read
Their consolations fill my heart, their wisdom feeds
    my head
Because they guide me, provide me, when I need
    escape they hide me
And my mind's made up yet opened up by so much
    that I've read

Their words are not enough to name the blessings
    that they bring
The wonder of their pictures or the songs their poems
    sing
And their prose by any other name would have
    as many flavours
So I can't think of a better thing to do
Than sail away between the pages

Drift away with every word
No matter if the book is
Theoretical or fanciful or practical or joyously absurd
Sail away between the pages
Set a course for new frontiers
And everything that never really mattered
    in the first place
Simply disappears

Tortoise

The
Tor
Toise
Reads
So
Slow
Ly
That
He
Ne
Ver
Gets
To
Fin
Ish
A

Mr Dougherty* Has Trouble with the Register...

Aneesa
Good morning, Mr. Broccoli

Brian
Good morning, Mr. Crockery

Chloe
Good morning, Mr. Documents

David
Good morning, Mr. Equity

Ella
Good morning, Mr. Factory

Furrukh
Good morning, Mr. Glossary

Grace
Good morning, Mr. Handkerchief

* "Dougherty" is an Irish name pronounced something like Dok-er-tee, although the 'k' sound is actually more like the 'ch' in "Loch Ness". Two of the names in this poem are names I've been called, in all seriousness, by well-meaning infants.

Hassan
Good morning, Mr. Italy
Imogen
Good morning, Mr. Jealousy

Jordan
Good morning, Mr. Kissagram

Kassandra
Good morning, Mr. Lottery

Lewis
Good morning, Mr. Mockery

Mary
Good morning, Mr. Nectarine

Neville
Good morning, Mr. Opposite

Olive
Good morning, Mr. Pottery

Paul
Good morning, Mr. Quality

Queenie
Good morning, Mr. Rockery

Robert
Good morning, Mr. Sloppily

Susie
Good morning, Mr. Trickery
Thomas
Good morning, Mr. Utterly

Uhura
Good morning, Mr. Vertical

Vincent
Good morning, Mr. Watery

Willow
Good morning, Mr. Xylophone

Xavier
Good morning, Mr. Yesterday

Yolanda
Good morning, Mr. Zebedee

Zain
Good morning, Mr. Adequate

And *Tamara*
Good morning, Mr. Dougherty.
(Hurrah!)
But my name isn't Tamara.
It's Tomato.

Auntie Fred

When I was just a little lad, a stranger came to stay
I didn't know her name, but still I liked her
    right away
Daddy scowled and Rover growled but Mummy
    calmly said
"Now, children, come and say hello to long-lost
    Auntie Fred."

My life has never been the same since Auntie Fred
    appeared
With her lingering smell of aftershave and bushy
    ginger beard
She read peculiar novels and she smoked her pipe
    in bed
You've never seen the like of my amazing
    Auntie Fred.

Oh, Auntie Fred, Auntie Fred
I don't know why you left us, was it something
    that I said?
Oh, Auntie Fred, Auntie Fred
I wish that you would come back, Auntie Fred.

My Mum demanded Auntie pay us something for
    her rent
Her room, her bed, her food and all the teaspoons
    that she bent
Now Auntie had no money, but she had a spot of luck
When she got herself a job as driver of a ten-ton truck.

I well remember Auntie in her favourite rocking chair
In the flowery dress and surplus army-boots she used to
    wear
And sometimes in the evenings in her voice so deep and
    gruff
She'd instruct me so precisely in the art of taking snuff.

Oh, Auntie Fred, Auntie Fred
I don't know why you left us, was it something
    that I said?
Oh, Auntie Fred, Auntie Fred
I wish that you would come back, Auntie Fred.

But then one fateful evening, a policeman came to call
My Auntie took one look at him and bolted down
    the hall

She battered down the kitchen door and up the lane
    she fled
And nothing more was seen of my amazing
    Auntie Fred.

So now my friends and neighbours can be seen to wear
    a frown
For Auntie's disappearance is a loss to all the town
And in the church, the organist can't think how to
    replace
The talents of the Parish Choir's unusual female bass.

Oh, Auntie Fred, Auntie Fred
I don't know why you left us, was it something
    that I said?
Oh, Auntie Fred, Auntie Fred
I wish that you would come back, Auntie Fred
I wish that you would come back, Auntie Fred
I wish that you would come back, Auntie Fred

2M and the Lion

There once was an enormous lion
Whose name was Miserable Ryan.
A beast both furious and wild
Whose favourite food of all was – child!

And so this lion fierce and cruel
One day arrived to hunt in school.
At every window, every door
He growled and gave a dreadful ROAR!

The children, sitting in assembly
Grew pale and cold and scared and trembly.
They all began to shake with fear
And shout, "Miss! There's a lion near!"

Miss Grimshaw, sighing with frustration
Said, "Goodness! What imagination!
There is no savage beast outside."
"There is! There is!" the children cried.

"Just look out through the window-pane!
You'll see its bushy golden mane!
You'll see its hungry yellow eyes!
We're scared, Miss! We're not telling lies!
It's not a fib! It's not a fake!

We're frightened! Can't you see us shake?"
Miss Grimshaw said, "Now don't be silly!
You're shivering because it's chilly.
Go back to class and find your teacher
And if you're frightened of this creature
Ask her to make it go away
Before she takes you out to play."

A lion hunting for a feast
Is really quite a clever beast.
And so, before the children came
To skip a rope or play a game
He crept, as quiet as a mouse
Behind the little wooden house
To lie in wait, as lions do
For children he could crunch and chew.

First, out came the reception classes.
"I can't see them without my glasses!"
He muttered. "They are *much* too small.
They wouldn't fill me up at all."

Next came Year One. "Humph! Still no good!
A snack, when I want filling food!"

Then came 2Q, led by Miss Quinney.
"Oh, no!" he moaned. "They're much too skinny!"

But finally, out came 2M.
"I think," he smiled, "that I'll eat – THEM!"
He crouched. He tensed. He bared each fang…
Then – Miserable Ryan sprang!
He landed right by poor Miss Howard
Who – though she's never been a coward –
Fainted. I think I would too
Faced with a lion. Wouldn't you?

This really rather angered Eleanor
(Especially as Miss Howard fell on her)
And so she furiously rose
And punched the lion on the nose.

Surprised, the lion gave a squeal.
"You horrid little Happy Meal!
Of all these children, you're the worst,"
He roared, "and so I'll eat *you* first!"
"Oh no you don't!" her friends replied.
They rushed at him from every side
Determined none of them should be
A lion's breakfast, lunch or tea.

And, while they kept him occupied
Song-ee, unnoticed, crept inside
The classroom, where she quickly got
Some spreaders and a little pot

Of glue. She took it out to Nikki
Who made the lion's paws so sticky
That, as he tried to pounce, he found
She'd stuck him firmly to the ground.

Then Elliot said, "Ian, quick!
Before the lion's paws unstick!
I think I know what we should do!"
He told him. Ian thought it through.
Then, just as fast as he could zoom
He ran off to the teachers' room
Where, drinking coffee with the staff
He found his teacher, Miss Metcalfe.

"Miss! Quick!" he cried, "I need your drink!
No time to talk! No time to think!
The children whom you hold so dear
Are all about to disappear!
Although I'm sure the beast will choose
To leave aside their coats and shoes
Unless we're quick, you'll find the rest in
An angry lion's large intestine!"

So saying, he grabbed the drink, and running
Back to Elliot, whose cunning
Scheme was surely worth a shot
He shouted, "Here! It's piping hot!

I've done my bit! Now you're the man
To carry out your clever plan!"

Just then, they heard a fearsome sound
As from the glue and from the ground
One paw came loose! Another! Three!
"Run!" someone shouted. "Scarper! Flee!"
But Elliot said not a word
And neither boy nor coffee stirred.
Then, as the beast in fury roared
He lifted high the cup, and poured.

The lion fell like someone dead,
The coffee running from its head.
"Hurrah!" the children cried. "Well done!
We fought the wicked beast – and won!"
Then Alasdair, and Alex too
Ran off to telephone the zoo
And asked the lion-keeping bloke
To fetch the beast before it woke.

But Anna wondered, "Is it right
To leave it as it is? It might
Escape some day, and then who knows
Who it might eat from head to toes?"

"You're right," Rosina said. "It's true.
There's only one thing we can do.

For one so fierce and temperamental
The only cure is something dental."
"Too true," the other children said
And, standing on the lion's head
As he lay helpless underneath
They all began to pull his teeth.

Poor Miserable Ryan! Now
He eats no meat at all, for how
Can any lion crunch a bone
Without a tooth to call his own?
No beef, no pork, no lamb, no bacon
Since by 2M his teeth were taken.
And worst of all, what drives him wild
Is this: What is the only child
He'll ever get the chance to eat?
The sticky jelly-baby sweet!

Goodnight Man

I'll sing you the story of the Goodnight Man
Settle down, my darling, settle down
I'll sing you the story of the Goodnight Man
Settle down, settle down

How by your bedside the night-watch he'll keep
Settle down, my darling, settle down
He'll slip in through your window the moment
    you're asleep
Settle down, settle down

He'll watch through the night with a light in his hand
To ward off the dragons from the darkness-land
And though your little eyes may never see
He'll always be there when you need him to be

The Goodnight Man is your Daddy's love
Settle down, my darling, settle down
The Goodnight Man is your Daddy's love
Settle down, settle down
Settle down

And even should your Daddy be far away
The Goodnight Man will be with you
Every night
And day.

John Dougherty

is a Northern Irish writer who now lives in
Gloucestershire. He worked as a primary school
teacher until 2004, when he became a full-time author.
His first book, *Zeus on the Loose*, was shortlisted for
the Branford Boase Award, and he is the author of the
hugely popular *Stinkbomb & Ketchup-Face* books for
primary-age children. John is former chair
of the UK Children's Writers and Illustrators
Group of the Society of Authors.
He is a popular performer in schools
and book festivals across the UK.